Zodiac Kids Your Starry Guide to Your Sign

Cancer

MINERVA OAKMONT

For all the young Cancers whose hearts are as deep as the ocean—may you always feel the courage to ride the waves of your emotions and the strength to share your incredible depths with the world. This book is dedicated to you, the sensitive dreamers and creative spirits who teach us the power of empathy and the beauty of caring deeply. May you always find magic in the moonlight and strength in the stars.

Book Cover by Tukotuku Publishing

Illustrations by Tukotuku Publishing

First edition 2025

Print ISBN: 978-1-991339-83-6

Ebook ISBN: 978-1-991339-84-3

Contents

Hey There, Future Astro Adventurers!

Get ready to dive into the splashy, emotional, and oh-so-cool world of Cancer! If you were born between June 21 and July 22, you're officially a member of the Cancer crew, known for being super caring, kinda crafty, and a wee bit moody. But that's what makes you amazing!

Imagine being able to feel what your friends are feeling without them saying a word—that's your superpower, Cancer pals! Your sign is like that friend who always has the best snacks and the biggest hugs, ready to cheer you up or celebrate your wins. And guess what? You're ruled by the Moon, which means you're in tune with your emotions like a pro surfer riding the waves of a gnarly sea.

Cancers are like the cozy blankets of the zodiac, always ready to snuggle up and keep things comfy. Whether you're watching your favorite movie for the zillionth time or building a fort in your living room, you know how to make everything feel just right. So buckle up, and get ready for a journey into the stars, where being a Cancer means being the heart and soul of the party—or the quiet night in. Let's explore the stars, uncover your Cancer secrets, and have loads of fun along the way!

Welcome to the World of Cancer

What Does It Mean to Be a Cancer?

B eing a Cancer means you're like a soft, squishy marshmallow in the middle of a campfire! Cancers are known for being super sensitive, nurturing, and a bit moody—like a crab that might snap at you if you poke it the wrong way! But don't worry, Cancers also have a big heart and love to take care of their friends and family. If you're a Cancer, you probably enjoy hugging your stuffed animals more than anything else and might cry during sad movies, even if it's just a cartoon about a lost kitten!

One of the coolest things about being a Cancer is that you belong to the Water element. Water is all about emotions, just like how a river flows and sometimes splashes around. Think of it this way: Cancers feel things deeply, like when you get a big wave of happiness or a little puddle of sadness. This makes Cancers super compassionate and understanding. If you ever need a shoulder to cry on or someone to share your ice cream with, your Cancer pals are the best at being there for you, just like a trusty old rubber ducky floating by in the bath!

Now, let's dive into who you can be best buddies with! Cancers get along great with other water signs like Scorpio and Pisces because they understand each other's feels. It's like having a secret club of emotion experts! They also vibe well with earth signs like Taurus and Virgo, who can help keep them grounded when they're floating in their sea of feelings. But sometimes, they might have a harder time with fire signs like Aries and Leo, who can be a bit too loud and fiery for their gentle, ways. It's like trying to mix oil and water—fun, but a little messy!

As a Cancer, you might be the artistic type, and that's totally awesome! Cancers are known for their creativity, so whether it's doodling in your notebook or putting on a puppet show, let those artistic juices flow like a waterfall! Your emotions can inspire some of the best stories and drawings, so don't be afraid to express how you feel. Remember, even the greatest artists had their moments of feeling blue or super happy, and that's what makes their work special. So grab your crayons and let your imagination splash around!

Lastly, let's talk about the Cancer symbol: the crab! Crabs may look tough on the outside, but they're really just hiding a soft, squishy inside, kind of like you! When you see a crab scuttling sideways, think of how Cancers sometimes take their time to come out of their shells. They might act a bit shy or cautious at first, but once they're comfortable, they show their true colors. So, if you're a Cancer, embrace your crabby side! It's perfectly okay to be sensitive and caring, and you should always celebrate what makes you unique—like that magical blend of water, emotions, and creativity that only a Cancer can bring to the world!

Meet the Crab

Your New Best Friend

Hey there, future crab pals! Have you ever felt a little shy or sensitive, like you might just crawl back into your shell? Well, you're in good company! Belonging to the Cancer zodiac sign makes you special! Cancers are known for being super caring and creative, just like a friendly beach animal who wants to share its favorite seashells with you. So, let's dive into the wonderful world of Cancers and discover why being a crab is just the best!

First things first, let's talk about the crab itself. Why a crab, you ask? Well, they are the ultimate home-bodies, and they love to carry their cozy shells around wherever they go. Just like crabs, Cancers tend to be nurturing and protective of their friends and family. They might seem a bit hard on the outside, but inside, they have a heart as soft as a marshmallow! So, if you ever need a shoulder to cry on, your Cancer mate are always ready with a hug, or maybe even a snack. Who knew crabs could be so sweet?

Now, let's splash into the water, because that's where our crabby buddies thrive! As a sign, Cancers feel things deeply, like how a sponge soaks up liquids. This means you might have a knack for understanding how others feel, which is a superpower in its own right! You can sense when someone is happy or sad, and you can often help them feel better just by being there. So, if your buddies are feeling blue, don't be afraid to show off your Cancer sensitivity—just like a crab offering a ride on its back!

When it comes to friendships, Cancers are known for being the best buddies around. They get along great with fellow signs like them, like Pisces and Scorpio, who share that same emotional depth. But they can also form strong connections with earth signs like Taurus and Virgo, who help keep their crabby dreams grounded. Just remember, even if you meet someone who seems a bit different, you might still find a friendship that's just as special as your favorite treasure from the ocean floor!

Finally, let's not forget about creativity! Cancers are like little artists at heart, always dreaming up new ideas and artistic projects. Whether it's drawing, painting, or even writing a funny story, your crabby imagination knows no bounds. So, gather your crayons and let your creativity flow like the waves of the sea! Remember, being a Cancer means you have a unique way of seeing the world, and that's something to celebrate. So go ahead, make your mark, and let the world see your beautiful crabby spirit shine!

Cancer Traits and Characteristics

The Sensitive Superpower

Hey there, little crabs! Welcome to the world of Cancer, where being sensitive is not just a trait – it's like having a superpower! Imagine if you could feel emotions like a superhero feels the wind in their cape. For us Cancers, emotions are our cape, and we can swoosh through feelings at lightning speed! You see, when things get a little too emotional, don't worry; it's not just you. It's us Cancers who have a special radar for feelings. We can sense when someone is sad or happy, even if they don't say a word. So, the next time you notice someone looking a bit down, remember you're like a superhero who can help them feel better with just a smile!

Now, let's chat about our watery element! Cancers are like the ocean, full of mystery and depth. Water is our secret weapon, and it means we can go with the flow. Just like a wave that can crash on the shore or gently lap at your toes, we can feel things deeply. But wait, there's more! Our elemental sign also means we're super creative. Cancers often love to draw, paint, or write stories. So, if you find yourself doodling during math class, don't fret! That's just your inner Cancer showing through. You're not just drawing; you're creating a world where emotions splash around like dolphins in the sea!

Let's dive into the world of friends! If you're a Cancer, you might notice that you have some special buddies who just get you. Cancers often click with other signs within their element, like Pisces and Scorpio. It's like having a jellyfish party where everyone floats along together, sharing their feelings! But don't be surprised if you sometimes connect with fiery signs like Leo or Sagittarius. It's like mixing ice cream with hot fudge – a little unexpected but totally delicious! Remember, it's all about finding friends who appreciate your thoughtful side and make you feel like the superstar you are!

Now, let's discuss the animal symbolism. Yep, that little crab that walks sideways is actually smarter than it looks. The crab represents our protective nature. Just like a crab hides in its shell when it feels scared, us Cancers sometimes pull back into our shells when things get tough. But here's the secret: we also have big hearts and lots of love to share! When we come out of our shells, we can be the life of the party, making everyone laugh with our silly jokes and fun stories. So, don't be shy – let your inner crab shine!

Finally, let's wrap it up with a splash of creativity! As a Cancer, you might find that you express your feelings through art. Whether it's painting, writing, or dancing like nobody's watching, let those emotions flow! Your creativity is your superpower, and the world needs your unique sparkle. So grab those crayons, write that story, or belt out your favorite song! Remember, being sensitive is not just okay; it's fabulous! Embrace your superpower, little Cancer, and show the world just how amazing it is to feel deeply and create freely!

Homebody or Adventurer?

When it comes to deciding whether you're a homebody or an adventurer, Cancers often find themselves juggling between cozy blankets and exciting escapades. Imagine curling up on your couch, surrounded by your favorite snacks, while your friends are off climbing mountains or exploring new cities. Sounds familiar, right? You're not alone! As a Cancer, you might feel like a crab stuck in its shell, perfectly content at home but also curious about what lies beyond your front door. The truth is, you can be both—a master of couch surfing and a fearless explorer of the great outdoors!

Now, let's talk about those cozy nights in. There's nothing better than snuggling up with a good book or watching movies that make you laugh, cry, or both! Cancers have a magical ability to turn any space into a warm and inviting sanctuary. You can create a fort out of pillows and blankets, complete with fairy lights and your favorite toys. Who needs a jungle gym when you have a blanket fort that doubles as a spaceship? But just when you think you've settled in for a long hibernation, your adventurous side starts to bubble up like a fizzy soda!

Picture this: one day, your besties are planning a fun day at the amusement park. You might feel a tug at your heart, wondering if you should stay in your cozy cocoon or jump out and join the fun. Cancers have a reputation for being sensitive, which means you can feel excited and nervous at the same time. But here's the secret—adventures can be a blast! You can channel your inner crab and scuttle out into the world, ready to discover new things while still sneaking back home for a snack later.

Cancers are like the ocean, where the waves can be calm and peaceful or wild and adventurous. Just like water can create beautiful waves, you have the power to ride both sides of the tide. Don't be afraid to dip your toes into new experiences. You might find that adventure is just as sweet as your favorite dessert! Plus, you can always bring your creative flair along for the ride. Whether it's sketching the sights you see or writing a story about your adventures, your imagination knows no bounds!

So, whether you prefer to be a homebody or an adventurer, remember that both sides of you are equally fantastic. The important thing is to embrace your feelings, explore when you're ready, and always carry a piece of home in your heart. After all, you are a Cancer, and your unique blend of sensitivity and adventure makes you shine like the brightest star in the night sky! So go ahead—snuggle up or explore the world, because as a Cancer, you truly can have the best of both worlds!

Mood Swings

The Roller Coaster Ride

M ood swings for Cancer kids can feel like a wild ride at an amusement park. One moment, you're as cheery as a cupcake, giggling with friends, and the next, you might feel like a balloon that just lost all its air. As a Cancer, you have a special knack for feeling all the feels, which can sometimes leave you dizzy, like you just got off a spinny ride that whirls you around and around. But guess what? This is perfectly normal for little crabs like you!

Think of your emotions as a swimming pool filled with water. Sometimes, the water is calm and serene, perfect for a nice, relaxing float. Other times, it can splash around like a big wave crashing on the shore. When you're feeling happy, it's like the sun is shining on your pool, making it sparkle. But when those mood swings hit, it can feel like a thunderstorm has rolled in, and you might want to hide under your blanket like a crab retreating into its shell. Just remember, after every storm comes a rainbow!

Now, let's talk about your superpower: being sensitive! This means you pick up on feelings around you like a sponge. If your friend is sad, you might feel that too, which can lead to your own mood taking a dive. But here's the cool part: your sensitivity allows you to create amazing art, write heartfelt stories, and even make your friends feel better. So when your emotions feel like a roller coaster, use that energy to express yourself! Grab some crayons or paint and let your mood flow onto the paper like water from a fountain.

Cancer kids are also known for their love of family and friendship. Sometimes, when you're feeling moody, a hug from a family member or a fun playdate with mates can turn that frown upside down. Think of your zodiac buddies: some signs like Taurus and Pisces might be great partners in your emotional adventure, while others, like fiery Aries, might make you feel a bit overwhelmed. Knowing who you click with can help you navigate those mood waves much better!

In the end, being a Cancer means you are on a fantastic journey through the ocean of emotions. It's like being a captain of a ship, sometimes sailing smoothly and sometimes facing a storm. Embrace your moods, share them with others, and don't be afraid to ride those mood swings like a pro. And remember, whether you're feeling like a joyful dolphin or a grumpy sea turtle, it's all part of being a wonderful, sensitive crab!

Cancer's Element

Water and Its Significance

Splish Splash! Why Water Matters

Hey there, little crabs! Get ready to dive into the wonderful world of water, because as a Cancer, it's your special element. Imagine a giant swimming pool filled with your favorite jellybeans—water is just as exciting! Water is not just for swimming; it's also the magical stuff that makes you feel all the feels. Just like the ocean can be calm one moment and wild the next, your emotions can take you on quite the ride. So grab your inner floaties, and let's explore why water matters for a Cancer kid like you!

First off, let's chat about what water does for us. It keeps us hydrated and our bodies happy, but it's also like a magical potion for your emotions. If you've ever felt like a water balloon ready to burst or a fish in a bowl feeling a bit lonely, you know exactly what I mean! Cancer kids are super sensitive, so when the waves of emotion crash, it can feel overwhelming. But guess what? Just like a cozy blanket can make you feel safe, water can help soothe those feelings. Next time you're feeling a little crabby, try splashing around in a pool or taking a long, relaxing bath. It's like giving your emotions a big, refreshing hug!

Now, let's get a little deeper—pun intended! Did you know that your connection with water makes you a creative genius? That's right! Think of all the amazing things you can do with water: painting with it, creating cool science experiments, or even making art with splashes and drips. Water encourages your imagination to flow like a river, and as a Cancer, your artistic side loves to express itself. Whether you're doodling or daydreaming, let the waves of creativity wash over you. Who knows, you might create something so fantastic that it could make even a crab dance!

Speaking of crabs, let's not forget about your zodiac symbol! Cancers are represented by the crab, which is known for its tough shell but soft insides. Just like a crab scuttles sideways in the sand, you might sometimes feel like you're moving in your own unique way, especially when it comes to friendships. Your sensitivity helps you connect deeply with others, but it can also make you a bit shy. Don't worry! Water helps you build those connections. Think of it like a secret sauce—when you share your feelings, your friendships can grow stronger, just like a plant needs water to thrive.

Finally, let's dive into compatibility! As a Cancer, you might find yourself clicking with other water signs like Scorpio and Pisces. They're like the perfect swimming buddies who understand your emotional waves. But don't forget the earth signs like Taurus and Virgo—they can help keep your boat steady when the waters get a little choppy. So whether you're splashing with friends or floating solo, remember that your water element is a treasure that helps you navigate through life. Embrace your sensitivity, let your creativity shine, and always keep swimming, little Cancer!

The Ocean of Emotions

The Ocean of Emotions is like a big, wavy playground for Cancers, and if you're born under this sign, you're probably the captain of the emotional ship! Imagine your feelings as a giant ocean, sometimes calm and sparkly, and other times stormy and wild. It's okay to surf those waves because Cancers are known for being super sensitive, like jellyfish that feel everything in the water around them. So, if you ever feel like you're on a roller coaster of emotions, just know that you're not alone. Every crab has its tides!

Now, let's dive into what makes Cancers so unique. You might have noticed that you care a lot about your friends and family, almost like you have a built-in radar for feelings. This is one of those super cool Cancer traits! While some kids might be busy playing games, Cancers are often off in their own world, thinking about how their mates are feeling.

It's like you have a special superpower that helps you understand others, but sometimes, it can feel like a little too much. Remember, it's totally okay to take a break from all those feelings and just chill on the beach for a bit!

Speaking of the beach, did you know that Cancers are ? Water is all about emotions, just like how a calm sea can suddenly turn into a big splashy wave! Cancers are like those ocean waves: sometimes smooth and peaceful, and other times, they crash with lots of feelings. Being a water sign means that you are deeply connected to your emotions, and you might find comfort in things like swimming, drawing, or even just daydreaming by a pond. So, the next time you feel a wave of emotions coming, just think about how water can shape the world!

Now, let's talk about who gets along best with our crabby friends. Cancers have special friendships with other signs, especially the ones that appreciate their sensitive side. Signs like Taurus and Pisces can be like cozy beach blankets on a chilly day, making you feel warm and understood. But watch out for signs that might be a bit too fiery, like Aries, who might make you feel like you're caught in a whirlpool! It's important to find peers who can swim with you through the emotional waves, so you can laugh, cry, and enjoy the ride together.

Finally, let's not forget that being a Cancer means you're likely to be super creative! Whether it's drawing, writing, or even making up silly songs about your feelings, there are endless ways to express your inner ocean. Creativity is like a magical boat that helps you sail through your emotions. So grab your paintbrush or your favorite musical instrument and let those feelings flow! Remember, every wave in your ocean is a part of who you are, and sharing them can make your world even brighter.

Riding the Waves of Feelings

R iding the waves of feelings is a whole lot like riding a roller coaster, but instead of loops and drops, it's all about the tidal waves of emotions! As a Cancer you might feel like you're swimming in an ocean of sympathy every day. One moment you're as happy as a dolphin jumping through the waves, and the next, you might feel like you're caught in a stormy sea! But don't worry; this is just part of your superpower as a Cancer. You're like a superhero of moods, ready to dive deep into emotional waters and come out shining like a pearl!

Being a Cancer means you're sensitive, and that's a good thing! Imagine having a super-duper radar that picks up everyone's feelings around you. While some kids might walk past a friend who's sad, you're the one who notices and feels like a big, warm hug is needed. It's like having a sixth sense, and while it can be overwhelming at times, it also helps you connect with your friends on a deeper level. Just remember, riding these waves means keeping your life jacket of self-care handy when the waters get a little rough!

Now, let's chat about your element: water! Water is pretty cool because it's always changing—sometimes calm, sometimes wild. Just like you! When you're feeling super creative, you might pour your emotions into art, music, or writing. But when the waves get too high, maybe it's time to splash around a little or chill out by the pool. Water reminds you that it's okay to feel everything from joyful splashes to deep, mysterious depths. So, grab your surfboard and ride those waves with style!

But wait, there's more to being a Cancer than just feeling all the moods! You're like a cozy blanket that fits perfectly with other signs like Pisces and Scorpio, who also swim in the waters of emotions. But watch out for those fiery signs like Aries and Leo; they might feel like a hot sunbeam on your cool underwater adventures. Finding mates who understand your emotional waves can make every day feel like a beach party!

So, as you ride the waves of feelings, don't forget to embrace your Cancer traits! You're not just sensitive; you're also nurturing, creative, and loyal. Think of yourself as a friendly crab, scuttling along the beach with your buddies and family. You have the power to create beautiful things from your emotions, and every splash of creativity adds color to your world. So, whether you're painting, writing, or just being your awesome self, keep riding those waves and let your emotions guide you on this fun adventure!

Cancer Compatibility with Other Zodiac Signs

Who's Your Zodiac Sidekick?

E ver wondered who your zodiac sidekick might be? Well, for all you imaginative little Cancers out there, your perfect partner-in-crime is none other than the wise and whimsical Pisces! Picture this: a dreamy fish swimming alongside your crabby self, navigating the ocean of life together. While you might prefer a cozy shell, Pisces loves to swim in the vast waters of creativity and imagination. Together, you can create magical adventures, whether it's building a sandcastle at the beach or hosting a tea party for your stuffed animals. Just make sure not to pinch them too hard when they make you laugh!

Now, let's dive into the ocean of emotions, shall we? As a Cancer, you're known for wearing your heart on your sleeve, which can sometimes feel like a soggy sleeve after a rainstorm. But don't worry! Your Pisces sidekick totally gets it. They can help you turn those emotional waves into beautiful art. Want to paint your feelings? Your Pisces buddy will be right there with you, splashing colors all over! Together, you can turn your sensitivity into a superpower, showing everyone that it's okay to feel deeply. Plus, you can always count on them for a good cry-fest over ice cream.

But wait! What about your other zodiac pals? Well, you might find that Taurus, with their earthy vibes, makes a great friend too. They'll help keep your dreams grounded, making sure you don't float away into the clouds during math class. On the other hand, your fiery Leo friends will ignite your creativity, encouraging you to perform in front of the class or whip up a inspiring project. Just remember, while Leos love the spotlight, you might prefer hiding in your cozy shell, and that's perfectly okay!

Now, let's not forget about the crab symbol! The crab represents your zodiac sign, and it's a pretty cool critter. Just like a crab, you might sometimes retreat into your shell when things get overwhelming. But here's the twist: crabs can also scuttle sideways, which means you're resourceful and clever! You can tackle your problems in adaptable ways, just like a crab finding its way around obstacles. So, if something's bothering you, don't be afraid to scuttle sideways until you figure it out. Your Pisces sidekick will be right there to cheer you on!

In the end, your zodiac sidekick is all about understanding, creativity, and a splash of fun! With your emotional depth and your sidekick's imaginative spirit, you can explore the world together, turning everyday moments into extraordinary adventures. Remember, being a Cancer means you're not just sensitive; you're also a fantastic friend, a budding artist, and a inspirational genius waiting to shine! So grab your Pisces buddy, and let the journey begin!

Best Buddies

Cancers and Their Fave Signs

Hey there, little star-gazers! Being a Cancer means you're not just any kid; you're a superstar with a crabby twist! Cancers are like the superheroes of the zodiac, equipped with a shell for protection and a heart that's as big as the ocean. You might find yourself daydreaming on a beach, building sandcastles, or swimming with dolphins! In this underwater world of emotions, Cancers are sensitive, caring, and super creative, making them the best buddies you could ever ask for.

As a Cancer, you might find that emotions are your secret superpower. Imagine being able to feel what others feel, almost like having a magical sixth sense! This sensitivity means you can make friends easily and have a knack for comforting others. However, it also means you might cry during sad movies or when your favorite ice cream flavor is sold out. But hey, that just makes you more relatable! Everyone loves a friend who can share a laugh one minute and a heartfelt moment the next. So, grab your tissues and let the feelings flow!

Now, let's dive into the watery world of Cancers! Water is your element, and just like the ocean, you can be calm and serene or a wild wave of emotions. This means you're adaptable and can go with the flow, but you might also feel a bit overwhelmed when things get too chaotic. Think of yourself as a gentle stream, winding through the forest, or a playful wave, splashing around at the beach. Just remember, it's okay to take a deep breath and float for a while when life gets a bit too splashy!

When it comes to friendship, you'll find that some signs are like peanut butter and jelly with you! Other water signs like Scorpio and Pisces totally get your vibe. They understand your emotional rollercoaster and can ride it with you. Earth signs like Taurus and Virgo can be great pals too, grounding you when you float too high in your feelings. Just be careful around fiery signs like Aries and Leo; they might set off your emotional spark in unexpected ways! But hey, opposites attract, right? So, let's mix it up and see what fun friendships can come from it!

And what about creativity? Cancers are born artists! Whether you're painting a masterpiece, writing a story, or dancing like no one's watching, your artistic flair is as bright as a shooting star. Use your emotions to fuel your creativity; let your feelings splash onto the canvas! So grab those crayons, unleash your imagination, and show the world the magical, crabby, and wonderfully sensitive person you are. Remember, being a Cancer means you're unique, and your feelings are like treasure waiting to be shared!

The "Uh-Oh" Signs

Compatibility Challenges

U h-oh! Every Cancer kid knows that some-times, friendships and relationships can feel a bit like a crab trying to walk in a straight line—just a little sideways and confusing! As the sensitive sea creatures of the zodiac, Cancer kids often find themselves swimming in a pool of emotions, and sometimes, those feelings can clash with others. When it comes to similarity, certain signs might make you feel like a cozy blanket, while others might feel like a prickly sea urchin. So, let's dive into some "uh-oh" signs that might pop up when your Cancer vibes meet other zodiac signs!

First up, we've got the fiery Aries. While they're adventurous and full of energy, they might sometimes leave you feeling like a soggy sponge! Aries loves to charge ahead, making plans and diving into new things, while you, dear Cancer, might be more of a "let's cuddle with our favorite movie" kind of buddy. If you find yourself feeling overwhelmed by their speed, it's okay to take a step back and say, "Whoa, slow down, my crabby friend!" Finding a balance between their fire and your can be a challenge, but with some humor and understanding, you might just find a way to enjoy each other's company.

Then there's the charming Libra. Those Libra kids are smooth talkers and lovers of fun, but they can be a bit indecisive. Imagine trying to play a game of rock-paper-scissors with someone who can't decide what to choose! You might feel a bit like a crab stuck in its shell, wanting to make plans but unsure where to go. If you're ever in a situation where your Libra friend is flipping a coin just to decide what ice cream flavor to get, remember that it's okay to be patient. Sometimes, you just need to bring out your inner artist and create a masterpiece of flavors yourself!

Now, let's talk about the grounded Earth signs like Taurus and Virgo. While they can be stable and reliable, sometimes they might appear a little too serious for your playful Cancer heart. You might find yourself wanting to splash around and play while they're busy organizing their snack collection. If they don't get your creative, emotional side, it might feel like you're trying to dance in a library! But with some fun games and fun activities, you can show them that emotions can be just as fun as counting snacks and organizing toys.

Lastly, we can't forget about the wild card, Sagittarius. They're adventurous and love to explore, but sometimes they can come off as a bit too free-spirited for your empathetic nature. Picture yourself wanting to build sandcastles while they're off chasing butterflies. If you ever feel like they're running circles around you, it's totally normal! Just remember that while they're busy exploring the world, you can stay connected by sharing your favorite stories and dreams. Who knows, maybe your storytelling will inspire their next big adventure!

In the end, dear Cancer kids, compatibility challenges are just like the waves of the ocean—sometimes they're calm, and other times they're a bit choppy. But don't worry! With your sensitivity, creativity, and a sprinkle of humor, you can navigate through these challenges and make wonderful connections with all the different signs. Remember, it's all about finding your rhythm, sharing laughter, and embracing the beauty of your unique crabby self!

Understanding Emotions

Cancer's Sensitivity

Crying Over Spilled Milk (Literally!)

C rying over spilled milk is a classic saying that most of us have heard, but for you little Cancers, it can feel like the end of the world! Imagine this: you knock over a glass of milk during breakfast, and in that moment, it's not just milk—it's your hopes and dreams of having a perfectly smooth morning. As a Cancer, you might find yourself feeling a wave of emotions, making the situation feel like a dramatic scene in a movie. But hey, it's just milk! So, let's dive into why you might feel so much and how to handle those watery emotions without swimming in a sea of tears.

As a Cancer, you are ruled by the element of water, which means your feelings can flow like a river or crash like a wave! When something doesn't go your way, like that spilled milk, it's totally okay to feel upset. In fact, you might feel it so deeply that it seems like a tidal wave of emotions! Embracing your sensitivity is important, and understanding that it's part of what makes you uniquely you can help. Remember, even the strongest crabs have soft bellies, and that's perfectly fine! So, the next time you feel like crying over spilled milk, take a deep breath and remind yourself that sometimes, it's just a little mess.

Now, let's talk about your crabby nature! The crab is your symbol, and it means you have a hard shell to protect your soft, squishy emotions inside. When you get upset, it's easy to retreat into your shell, wishing the world would just leave you alone. But here's a fun fact: crabs are also great at building homes! Instead of hiding, why not create a little art project to express how you feel? Grab some crayons, a piece of paper, and draw your feelings about that spilled milk! Who knows, you might just inspire others with your creativity, showing that it's okay to let moods flow out in colorful ways.

Speaking of creativity, your sensitivity is a superpower that can make you an amazing artist!

When you feel deeply, you can turn those feelings into beautiful artwork, stories, or even music. This means the next time you spill something (or someone spills it for you), grab your art supplies and let those emotions out! Whether it's painting a picture of a milk splash or writing a funny poem about how your morning went wrong, channeling your feelings into creativity can make you feel better and might even make others smile.

Finally, let's explore how you get along with other signs. As a Cancer, you are known for being nurturing and caring, making you a great friend to many signs. However, some signs might not understand your sensitivity right away. If a fiery Leo laughs at your milk mishap, don't take it too personally! Remember, every sign has its strengths and weaknesses. Finding friends who appreciate your sensitive side will help you feel more comfortable. So, next time you knock over your juice, laugh it off, and maybe even invite your mates to join you in creating a funny story about it. Remember, it's just milk, and life is too short to dwell on spills!

Building Emotional Fortresses

B uilding emotional fortresses is like building a cozy fort made of pillows and blankets, but instead of keeping out monsters, it helps you protect your feelings! As a Cancer, your emotions can be as deep as the ocean, and sometimes they feel like a tidal wave crashing over you. But don't worry! With a little creativity and your trusty crab shell, you can create a safe space to express and manage those moods. Think of your emotions as a wild ocean; sometimes it's calm, and other times it's a bit stormy. It's totally normal to feel like your heart is a squishy jellyfish when things get tough!

Now, let's talk about your crabby side! Cancers are known for their ability to retreat into their shells when they need a break. Imagine you're a crab, scuttling away from the noise of the world to your cozy shell. That shell is your emotional fortress! When you feel overwhelmed, it's okay to take a little time to recharge. This might mean spending time with your favorite book, doodling in your sketchbook, or even just daydreaming about swimming in your own magical underwater kingdom. Remember, your fortress is a place where you can feel safe and loved.

You might also notice that your crab shell has some pretty cool decorations. Just like your favorite ornaments, your feelings can be colorful and unique! Some days you might feel like a bright, sunny day, while other days may feel like a rainy afternoon. Embracing all those colors is what makes you special. Your friends might not get it, but that's okay! They can be like the jellyfish, floating around, while you're the wise crab, navigating the waves of emotions. And when you let your emotions out, it can be like a beautiful underwater dance party!

Let's talk about how close a Cancer can be with other signs! Some signs get along like peanut butter and jelly, while others may feel a little more like oil and water. As a Cancer, you might find that fellow water signs understand your emotional depth. But don't worry if you're best buddies with a fiery Leo or a bubbly Gemini; sometimes opposites attract! It's all about finding those who respect your feelings and don't mind when you need a little extra time in your shell. Remember, every good castle has a few loyal knights to protect it!

Finally, let's not forget the imaginative side of being a Cancer! Your emotions are like a treasure chest full of inspiration waiting to burst out. Whether you love painting, writing, or even acting, let your feelings flow into your art. When you express yourself, it's like building a bridge between your emotional fortress and the outside world. So grab your paintbrush, write a story, or put on a play about a crab who saves the day! Your creativity can help you connect with others and show them just how amazing and colorful your world can be. And who knows, maybe your emotional fortress will inspire others to build their own!

The Power of Empathy

Imagine a big, squishy crab scuttling along the beach, pinching at the sand with its tiny claws. That's the Cancer sign, and just like our crustacean buddy, people born under this sign are known for their strong s and emotions. But here's the twist: these affections are like a superpower! When Cancers feel something, they feel it deeply, like they've just taken a big gulp of ocean water. Empathy is the special ability that allows them to understand and share the warmths of others, making them the ultimate emotional detectives. So, if you're born under Cancer, you might be the friend who always knows when someone's feeling sad or happy, even if they don't say a word.

Now, let's think about the element of water, which is Cancer's favorite thing! Water is all about flow, depth, and sometimes a little bit of splash. Just like a river, Cancers can be calm and soothing or wild and unpredictable. When Cancers dive into their emotions, they can swim around with great ease, picking up on what others are going through like a sponge. This ability helps them connect with friends and family, making sure everyone feels understood. So, if you ever need a shoulder to cry on or someone to celebrate with, a Cancer is like the best life raft you could ask for!

But wait, there's more! Cancers are not just sensitive; they're also super creative! They can turn their emotions into amazing art, stories, or even songs. Think about it: have you ever heard a song that made you cry or feel all warm and fuzzy? That's the power of empathy at work! Cancers can take their emotional experiences and create something beautiful from them, like a painter with a magical brush that captures all the colors of their feelings. So, if you're a Cancer, don't be afraid to grab those crayons and let pour your heart out on paper!

Now, let's get to the fun part: Cancers talent with other signs! Cancers are like jellybeans—they get along great with certain flavors. They often make wonderful friends with other water signs, because they totally get each other's emotional waves. But they also can vibe with earth signs, like Taurus and Virgo, who can help keep them grounded. It's like having a buddy who gets your artistic side while also reminding you to finish your homework. Who wouldn't want a friend like that?

Finally, let's not forget the crab symbol. This little creature is tough on the outside but soft on the inside, just like you might be as a Cancer. It's a reminder that being sensitive is a strength, not a weakness. So, embrace your inner crab, and let the world see your unique gifts! Whether you're painting a picture, writing a story, or just being there for a friend, your empathy is a treasure. So grab your crayons, find your ocean, and let your creativity shine!

Cancer Symbolism

The Crab and Its Meaning

What's Up with the Crab?

W hat's up with the crab? Well, if you're a Cancer, you might just be as cozy as a crab in its shell! You see, the crab is the of the Cancer zodiac sign, and just like our little shellfish friend, Cancers are known for being protective and a bit shy. Imagine a crab scuttling sideways on the beach, always on the lookout for a safe spot to hide. That's a bit like Cancer kids, who often have big hearts but may take time to come out of their shells and show their true colors. So, if you ever find a Cancer kid hanging back at a party, don't worry—they're just making sure the coast is clear before they join in the fun!

Cancers are ruled by the element of water, which is pretty fitting considering how much they love to dive deep into their emotions. Water is all about emotions, and Cancers can be like little emotional oceans. Sometimes, they might feel like they're riding the waves, and other times, they could be feeling a bit stormy. But that's okay! Just like the ocean has its calm days, Cancers can also find their peaceful moments. If you have a Cancer buddy, you might notice they can cry during a sad movie or get super excited about happy news, proving that they feel everything deeply. So, next time you see a Cancer being a bit moody, remember they're just a water creature navigating their emotional tides!

Now, let's talk about how compatible a Caner is! Cancers tend to get along best with other signs who totally understand their emotional vibes. It's like they're all swimming in the same pool of emotions! But they can also be great friends with earth signs like Taurus and Virgo. Why? Because these earth signs help ground the emotional waves, creating a perfect balance. So, if you're a Cancer, look out for those special friendships where you can laugh, cry, and share snacks together. And if you ever feel a little crabby, just remember that a good buddy can make all the difference!

One of the coolest things about being a Cancer is your creativity! Many Cancer kids are super artsy, whether they love to draw, paint, or even write stories. Their imaginations are like treasure chests overflowing with colorful ideas. Plus, since they feel so much, they can turn their emotions into beautiful art. Encourage your Cancer friend to express themselves—maybe they'll create a masterpiece that makes everyone laugh or even cry happy tears. Remember, art is a fantastic way to share emotions, and Cancers are natural-born artists just waiting to shine!

So, what's the deal with the crab? The crab is not just a symbol; it's a reminder of how special Cancers are. They have a unique ability to feel deeply, create beautifully, and build strong connections with those around them. Whether they're hiding in their shells or splashing about in the emotional waters, Cancers are always ready to show love and friendship. So next time you see a crab, give it a wink and remember that it represents all the wonderful, sensitive, and artistic qualities that make being a Cancer truly awesome!

Shells and Softness

The Dual Nature

Shells and softness are like the best of friends for Cancer kids. Just like a crab, which has a hard shell to protect its squishy insides, you Cancerians have a tough outer layer that keeps your sensitive feelings safe. Imagine being a crab in a giant ocean, where the waves can be super splashy and unpredictable! But your shell is not just there to keep you safe; it shows the world that you can be strong, even when you feel like a jellyfish inside. So, when someone sees your crabby exterior, they might not realize that you're a big bundle of emotions, ready to share your creativity and kindness.

Now, let's dive into the watery world of Cancer! Water is your magical element, and it's not just for swimming pools or splashing around in the rain.

Water is all about emotions and passions, and as a Cancer, you're like a walking fountain of creativity and imagination. When you feel happy, it's like a bubbly brook, and when you're sad, it can feel like a heavy rainstorm. Understanding this watery connection helps you express your emotions better. So grab your paintbrush or your musical instrument, and let those feelings flow like a river!

Speaking of feelings, being a Cancer means you're super sensitive. And that's totally okay! You might cry during a sad movie or feel a bit shy when meeting new friends, but that just shows how much you care. It's like having a heart that's as big as the ocean! Remember, being intuitive is not a weakness; it's a strength. It allows you to connect with others and understand how they feel too. Ff someone is feeling blue, you can be their sunshine by simply being there for them. Your soft heart is a treasure, and it makes you a fantastic friend.

Now, let's talk about how you get along with other zodiac signs. Some signs are like peanut butter and jelly with you, while others might be more like oil and water. For example, you might find that you click well with Pisces and Scorpio, who also swim in the deep waters of emotions. But when it comes to fiery signs like Aries or Leo, it might feel like trying to mix water and fire! Understanding these relationships can help you make friendships that feel as cozy as a warm blanket on a rainy day.

Finally, the crab is your , and it has a special meaning! It reminds you to embrace both your strength and your softness. Just like a crab can scuttle sideways, you can navigate the world with your unique style. So, whether you're drawing, writing stories, or just daydreaming, let your imagination roam free! Your Cancer traits make you clever and kind, and the world needs more of that. So go ahead, be that artistic crab who expresses feelings through all sorts of fun ways, and remember, it's okay to show your soft side!

Crabby or Cute?

The Truth About Cancers

rabby or cute? That's the big question when it comes to Cancers! If you're a Cancer, you might have noticed that people can sometimes think you're a little bit crabby. But hold on! It's not all pinch and grumpiness. Cancers are known for being super sensitive and caring, kind of like a big fluffy pillow that also has a crab shell. So, if someone says you're crabby, just flash them your cutest smile and remind them that underneath that shell, you're actually a softie who just wants to be loved!

Now let's dive into the watery world of Cancers! Did you know that Cancer is a water sign? That means you're like a magical mermaid or merman who feels everything deeply—just like the ocean. Water flows and changes, and so do your emotions! Sometimes, you might feel as stormy as a hurricane, while other times, you can be as calm as a gentle wave. It's important to remember that being considerate is your superpower. It's what allows you to connect with your friends and family on a deeper level, making you the perfect listener and friend.

Speaking of friends, let's talk about who gets along best with our beloved Cancers! You might have heard that some zodiac signs are best buddies while others are like oil and water. Together, you can create a magical underwater world filled with laughter and creativity! On the other hand, fire signs like Aries and Leo might seem a little too hot for your cool, watery nature. But don't worry! With a little understanding, even those fiery guys or gals can learn to appreciate your unique charm.

The crab represents you, Cancer, and it's more than just a sea creature. It's even better! Crabs have hard shells to protect their soft interiors, just like you might put up walls to shield your feelings. But here's the fun part: crabs can also scuttle sideways, which means you might approach situations in your own special way. Instead of going straight for what you want, you might take a few side steps to figure things out first. That's just part of your charm and creativity!

And speaking of creativity, Cancers are often natural artists! You might find joy in drawing, painting, or even writing stories. This artistic expression is not just a hobby; it's a way for you to share your feelings with the world. So, the next time you feel a wave of emotions crashing over you, grab some crayons, paint, or a notebook and let your creativity flow. Remember, being a Cancer means you have a creative spirit that can turn even the stormiest feelings into beautiful art! So go ahead, embrace your inner crab, and let your cute and crabby self shine!

Personalized Cancer Horoscopes for Kids

Your Very Own Cancer Horoscope!

Welcome to your very own Cancer horoscope, where we dive into the watery world of emotions, creativity, and a dash of crabby humor! As a Cancer, you are like the ultimate friend who always remembers your birthday and brings cookies, but also sometimes hides in their shell when things get a little too wobbly. You're sensitive, sweet, and a tiny bit mysterious—just like a treasure chest at the bottom of the ocean! So, let's explore what makes you, well, you, and how the stars can make your day a little brighter.

First off, let's talk about your unique traits! Cancers are known for being nurturing, caring, and a little bit of a homebody. You probably love snuggling up with your favorite blanket, binge-watching your favorite shows, or creating art that paints your feelings. Remember, it's okay to cry during a sad movie—your tears are just your emotional superpower! Embracing your sensitivity means you understand others better, and that makes you one of the best friends anyone could ask for. Just like a superhero, you can feel things deeply, and that's what makes you special.

Now, let's splash into the element of water! As a water sign, you have a natural connection to your feelings, like a fish swimming in a sea of emotions. Water can be calm and soothing, like a gentle wave, or it can be wild and splashy, just like a surprise rainstorm! This means you might feel happy one minute and a little teary the next, and that's absolutely okay! Your emotional waves help you connect with others and understand how they feel, making you a true empathetic buddy. Just remember, even the ocean has its storms, but there's always a sunny day waiting to break through!

Did you know you're also a great match with Earth signs like Taurus and Virgo? They are the ones who help ground you when you're floating too high in your dreamy world. But watch out for those fiery signs like Aries and Leo—they can be a little too loud for your gentle spirit! Finding friends who understand your feelings and creativity will help you shine like the brightest star in the sky!

Lastly, let's celebrate your ingenuitive side! Cancers are often artistic and love to express themselves through drawing, writing, or even dancing around the living room like nobody's watching. Your sensitivity fuels your imagination, making your creations come alive with emotion. So, grab your paints, crayons, or even a journal, and let your feelings flow! Whether it's a masterpiece or a funny doodle of a crab in a party hat, remember that your creativity is a fantastic way to share your unique Cancer spirit with the world. Now, go out there and make your very own Cancer magic!

Fun Predictions for a Fun Day

G et ready for a fun day full of giggles and surprises, Cancer pals! If you're born under the sign of Cancer, you might know that you're a bit like a crab—tough on the outside but super soft on the inside. That means you have a special talent for feeling all the emotions you may be going through! So, let's dive into some predictions that promise a day filled with laughter, creativity, and maybe a few happy tears. Grab your imaginary crab claws, and let's scuttle along!

First up, expect a day where your creativity shines brighter than a shiny seashell on the beach. Maybe you'll create a masterpiece that makes your friends go "Wow!" or write a story that takes everyone on a wild underwater adventure. Keep those artistic juices flowing, and don't be afraid to use all the colors in the crayon box! Remember, your sensitive side helps you see the world in unique ways, so let that imagination swim free. Who knows? You might just invent a new superpower for crabs!

Next, let's talk about some fun encounters with your friends. Cancers are known for being great buddies, and today, you might find someone who needs a little extra love. Maybe a friend is feeling down, and you'll just know how to cheer them up with your funny jokes or silly dance moves. Just like a crab sharing its favorite rock, your kindness can make someone's day brighter. And if you happen to get into a silly competition of who can make the best crab dance, you might just discover you have some secret moves that would make any crab proud!

Now, let's make a splash with some watery fun! Since you're a water sign, you might feel extra energized when you're around water. This could mean a trip to the pool, a splashy water balloon fight, or even just a crazy science experiment with water at home. Just remember to have a towel nearby because we all know things can get messy! Let the water inspire you to think big and dream even bigger. After all, who knows what kind of sea creatures you might invent while splashing around?

As the day wraps up, you might want to take a moment to reflect on all the fun you had. Being a Cancer means you're in touch with your emotions, and today is no different. Write down your favorite moments in a journal or share them with your family at dinner. And if you feel a little teary-eyed while remembering the day, that's okay! Those subtle feelings are what make you uniquely you. Embrace that crabby heart of yours, and remember: it's perfectly fine to show your emotions.

So there you have it! A day filled with creativity, friendship, watery adventures, and heartfelt moments awaits you. Enjoy every second and let your Cancer spirit shine brighter than the sun sparkling on the ocean waves. Whether you're painting, dancing, splashing, or sharing, you're sure to have a blast. Now, go out there and make some magical memories—after all, the world is your oyster!

Making Sense of the Stars

Hey there, young star gazers! Have you ever looked up at the night sky and wondered what those twinkling stars are all about? Well, let me introduce you to a special constellation that's just for you — it's called Cancer! Now, before you start thinking about giant crabs invading your dreams, let's dive into the magical world of your astrological sign. Cancer is not only about crabs; it's about being super sensitive, caring, and creative. So grab your imaginary telescope and let's explore!

First up, let's talk about what it means to be a Cancer. You're a part of the Cancer crew, and that means you have some unique traits that make you shine like a supernova. Cancers are known for being nurturing, intuitive, and yes, a little moody at times (but who isn't?). It's like having a superpower when a friend is feeling down; you can sense their emotions and help lift their spirits. Just remember, with great sensitivity comes great responsibility—like not crying during sad movies!

Now, let's splash around in the element of water, which is the secret sauce of your sign. Water is all about emotions, creativity, and flowing with life. Think of it as being like a river: sometimes calm and peaceful, other times a wild splashy waterfall! As a Cancer, your empathy can run deep like the ocean, making you one of the most original signs. Whether you love painting, dancing, or writing cool stories, that watery energy helps you express yourself in amazing ways. So, if you ever feel a burst of inspiration, just know that it's the water magic kicking in!

How about friends? Cancers are great at making buddies, but not everyone gets along with our crabby pals. Earth signs like Taurus and Virgo can also be good matches since they provide stability, like a cozy rock in the middle of a gentle stream. Just be careful with fire signs like Aries or Leo; they can be a bit too fiery for your chill vibe. Remember, it's all about finding that perfect balance in your friendship circle!

Lastly, let's get to the heart of the matter—your emotions! As a Cancer, you might feel things more deeply than others. That's totally okay! It's like having a super-sensitive radar that picks up on feelings. Just remember to express those emotions creatively, and don't be afraid to share your emotions with friends and family. Whether you feel happy, sad, or just a bit crabby, talking about it can help. So, next time you find yourself feeling like a crab trapped in a shell, just take a deep breath and let your creativity flow like the waves of the ocean. You're not alone, and the stars are always shining bright just for you!

Cancer and Creativity

Encouraging Artistic Expression

The Creative Cancer: An Artful Adventure

If you're a Cancer, you might be wondering why your astrological sign is represented by a crab. Well, it's because crabs are super cool! They're tough on the outside but a little softie on the inside, just like you. You might be a sensitive soul who loves to express yourself through art, and that's totally awesome. Just like a crab scuttling sideways, you can explore your creativity from all angles, making art an exciting journey filled with laughter and joy!

Now, let's talk about emotions. As a Cancer, you might feel things a little more deeply than others. Imagine you're watching a sad movie, and your friends are all munching popcorn, but you're the one with tears streaming down your face. Yep, that's the Cancer superpower! You can feel happy, sad, excited, and even confused all at once. This sensitivity is like a paintbrush in your hand, allowing you to create masterpieces that capture all those feelings. So, grab your crayons and let your heart spill out onto the page, because your emotions can turn into some truly amazing art!

Water is the element of Cancer, and it's pretty significant. Think about how water can be calm and peaceful like a gentle stream or wild and splashy like a roaring ocean. As a Cancer kid, you might feel like you're riding the waves of your emotions. Sometimes, you'll want to dive deep into your creativity, like a dolphin leaping through the waves, while other times you might feel like curling up in your cozy shell. Embrace those feelings, and let them guide your artistic adventures. Just remember, even the biggest waves eventually settle down, and so can your emotions!

Now, let's chat about friends! It's like having a secret club of sensitivity and creativity when they're with other water signs! But you can also be friends with other signs too, like Leo and Virgo, who appreciate your artistic flair and kindness. Just think of all the amazing art projects you could do together! Whether you're making a giant mural or crafting friendship bracelets, the magic of collaboration can turn ordinary moments into extraordinary memories.

Finally, let's celebrate your inner artist! You might not know it yet, but you have a talent for bringing beauty to the world. Whether it's through drawing, painting, writing stories, or even dancing around your room, your creativity is like a treasure chest waiting to be unlocked. So, don't be shy about expressing yourself! Your unique perspective as a Cancer kid can inspire others, and who knows? You might just create the next big masterpiece that makes everyone smile. So, let's embark on this artful adventure together, and remember: the world is your canvas!

Writing, Drawing, and Dreaming Big

Writing, drawing, and dreaming big are like the ocean waves that Cancer kids ride on every day! You see, being a Cancer means you're a natural-born artist, a storyteller, and a daydreamer all rolled into one. Imagine a crab holding a paintbrush in one claw and a journal in the other, ready to create masterpieces about all the cool stuff in its underwater world. Cancers have a special gift for expressing their feelings, and this often comes out in their art, writing, and imagination. So, grab your crayons and let's dive into this imaginative sea!

Now, let's talk about Cancer traits! You're not just any ordinary crab; you're a super-sensitive, caring, and sometimes a bit moody little creature. It's like your emotions are a giant wave that can crash over you unexpectedly. But that's okay! Being sensitive means you can feel things deeply, which makes you a fantastic writer. You can bring your feelings to life with words, or paint the world with colors that show how you feel. Just remember, even the biggest waves calm down, and so can your emotions when they get too overwhelming!

Since Cancers are ruled by the element of water, it's no wonder that creativity flows easily for you. Think of yourself as a little fish swimming through a sea of imagination, where every thought can turn into a story or a drawing. Water is all about emotions, and when you let your feelings wash over you, the best ideas pop up like bubbles! So, whether you're splashing paint on canvas or scribbling in your journal, remember that your watery nature gives you the power to express yourself in unique and colorful ways.

Now, how do you get along with other zodiac signs while you're busy being creative? Cancers are the friendly crabs who love to hang out with others. You might find that you get along especially well with fellow water signs like Pisces and Scorpio. Together, you can create amazing art or write epic stories that dive deep into emotions. Don't forget about the earth signs like Taurus and Virgo; they can help keep your dreams grounded while you're off in your creative clouds. Just remember, it's all about sharing your creativity and having fun to-gether!

Lastly, let's not forget about the fun of personal-ized Cancer horoscopes! Imagine a special mes-sage just for you, saying how your creativity will shine this week. Maybe it's a great time to write that story about a crab superhero or draw a picture of your dream underwater castle. Whatever it is, let your imagination run wild! So, grab your pencil, open your mind, and let the waves of creativity wash over you. Remember, you're a magical Can-cer, and the world is your canvas!

Showcasing Your Inner Artist!

S howcasing your inner artist is like being a crab with a paintbrush! As a Cancer, you've got a special talent for turning your feelings into fantastic art. Whether it's drawing, painting, or even creating cool crafts, your imagination is as deep as the ocean. So grab those crayons, markers, or any crafty thing you can find because it's time to let your inner crab out of its shell! Remember, every masterpiece starts with a scribble, so don't be afraid to make a mess. Your unique artistic flair is something to celebrate, not hide!

Being a Cancer means you might feel things more deeply than your friends, and that's super cool! You have a knack for turning your emotions into beautiful creations. If you're feeling happy, paint a sunny picture. If you're blue, maybe a moody masterpiece is in order. Your emotions are like colors on a canvas, and each one can help you express what's happening inside. So next time you find yourself moody a bit crabby, grab that paintbrush and let your feelings flow. Who knows, you might just create the next great work of art!

Now, let's talk about your special water element. Just like a river or a flowing stream, your creativity can adapt and change! Water is all about movement, and so is your imagination. You can dive deep into different ideas and swim through creative currents that lead you to amazing places. Want to create a story about a magical underwater world? Go for it! Or maybe a comic strip about a crab superhero? Dive right in! Just remember, like water, your creativity can take many forms, so don't be afraid to splash around.

And guess what? Being a Cancer means you can connect with other signs too! Imagine working together with a Pisces friend to create a mural that tells a story through your art! Or maybe you can team up with a Leo to put on a fun play. It's like mixing colors on a palette – together, you can create something even more vibrant than you could alone. So reach out to your friends, and let's see what amazing things you can make together!

Lastly, remember that being sensitive is a super-power, not a weakness. Your ability to feel deeply can lead you to create art that touches others' hearts. Embrace your inner artist, and let it shine brightly! Whether it's through drawings, stories, or even dance, your creativity is a reflection of who you are. So, gather your supplies, unleash your imagination, and show the world the beauty of your Cancer creativity. You're not just a crab; you're a crab with a colorful, artistic personality ready to take on the world!

And That's a Wrap

On our starry adventure through the world of Cancer!

If you've sailed through this book, you now know that being a Cancer is pretty special. You're not just any star in the sky; you're a shining moonbeam that lights up the night with creativity and deep feels.

Cancers are like the superheroes of the emotional world. With your superpower of sensitivity, you can pick up on vibes and feelings that others might miss. This makes you an awesome friend who always knows when to offer a hug or share a giggle. And let's not forget about your creativity! Whether you're drawing, crafting, or spinning tales, you bring magic into everything you do, turning simple ideas into treasures.

But the most important thing to remember? Your feelings are your strength, not your kryptonite. They make you kind, empathetic, and totally unique. So, never shy away from showing who you really are. The world needs more Cancers to make it a warmer and more understanding place!

Keep exploring the stars, keep dreaming big, and keep being you—because the world is way more colorful and fun with Cancers like you in it. Grab your emotional toolbox and your creative gear, and prepare to make waves that will ripple far beyond your own little pond. Who knows? Maybe one day, you'll change the world just by being your awesome Cancer self!

Let's Meet Minerva

M inerva Oakmont is a young entrepreneur with a cosmic twist. A self-proclaimed astrology enthusiast, Minerva doesn't make a single move without consulting her chart—her secret weapon for thriving in both business and life. And thrive she does! With several flourishing, soul-centered businesses under her belt, she's rewriting the rules of entrepreneurship with heart and intuition.

Minerva isn't your typical businesswoman. With her vibrant purple, pink, and blue hair, she lives her life in full technicolor. When she's not making moves in the business world, you'll find her running marathons, practicing self-care, and hanging out with her gentle giants—her Great Danes and mastiff dogs. Together, they roam the magical woods behind her enchanted home, where inspiration flows like stardust.

Minerva's philosophy? Life is an adventure, and with the stars as her guide, she's determined to make every moment unforgettable.